W9-CBM-244

South America

By Allan Fowler

Consultant
Linda Cornwell
Coordinator of School Quality and Professional Improvement
Indiana State Teachers Association

Children's Press®
A Division of Grolier Publishing
New York   London   Hong Kong   Sydney
Danbury, Connecticut

Visit Children's Press® on the Internet at:
http://publishing.grolier.com

Designer: Herman Adler Design Group
Photo Researcher: Caroline Anderson
The photo on the cover shows Angel Falls, a waterfall in the South
American country of Venezuela.

Library of Congress Cataloging-in-Publication Data

Fowler, Allan.
    South America / by Allan Fowler.
        p. cm. — (Rookie read-about geography)
    Includes index.
    Summary: A simple introduction to the geographic features, people,
and animals of the continent of South America.
    ISBN 0-516-21672-4 (lib. bdg.)   0-516-27300-0 (pbk.)
    1. South America—Juvenile literature. 2. South America—
Geography—Juvenile literature. [1. South America.] I. Title. II. Series.
F2208.5.F69   2001
980—dc21
                                                    00-026023

GROLIER
PUBLISHING
            3 4 5 6 7 8 9 10 R 10 09 08 07 06 05 04 03 02

The biggest pieces of
land on Earth are called
continents.

There are seven continents.

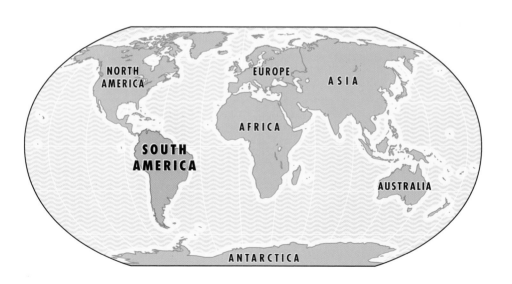

Crowded cities and thick
rain forests cover the
continent of South America.

The tall Andes (AN-deez) Mountains stretch up and down the land.

You can find South
America on a globe.

The top part of South
America is very wide.

The bottom part is narrow.

The Amazon River crosses
the wide part of the continent.
It begins in the country of
Peru (puh-ROO) and flows
into the Atlantic Ocean.
It carries more water than
any other river in the world.

The Amazon River

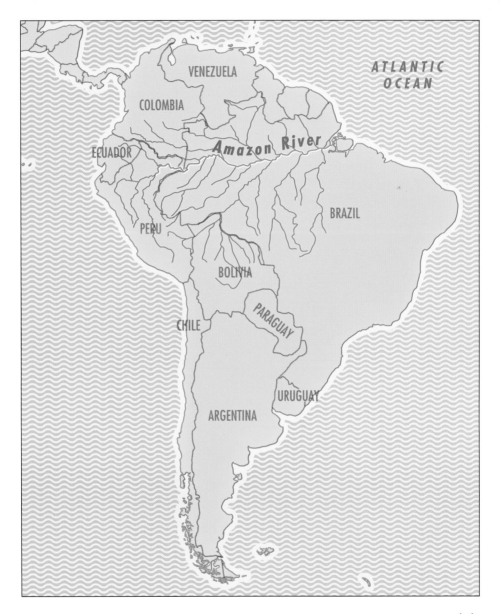

ATLANTIC OCEAN

VENEZUELA

COLOMBIA

Amazon River

ECUADOR

BRAZIL

PERU

BOLIVIA

PARAGUAY

CHILE

URUGUAY

ARGENTINA

11

The world's biggest rain forest grows on the land around the Amazon River.

It covers a large part of a country called Brazil.

Every day, many trees
are cut down in the rain
forest. The animals that
live there lose their homes.

Farms, cattle ranches,
and towns take the place
of the rain forest.

Brazil is the biggest country in South America. The city of Rio de Janeiro (REE-o day zhuh-NAIR-o) is in Brazil.

Sugarloaf Mountain rises high above Rio's beautiful beaches.

People in Brazil speak a language called Portuguese (poor-chuh-GEEZ).

In most other South American countries, people speak Spanish.

Colombia is a South American country where coffee beans grow.

Coffee beans

A cacao tree

Cacao (ka-KOW) grows
in the country of Ecuador
(EK-wuh-door). Chocolate
is made from cacao.

The pampas are flat, grassy lands in the country of Argentina (ar-jen-TEE-nah).

Cowboys called gauchos
(GOW-chose) work on
cattle ranches there.

Angel Falls is the world's highest waterfall. It is in the country of Venezuela (ven-uh-ZWAY-luh).

This waterfall tumbles more than three thousand feet.

Many kinds of animals live
in South America. Llamas
(LA-muhs) live in the
Andes Mountains.

Jaguars (JAG-wahrs) prowl the rain forests.

Macaws (muh-KAWS) and many other colorful birds brighten the trees and sky.

If you visit South America, you can see all of these wonderful things!

Words You Know

Amazon River

Andes Mountains

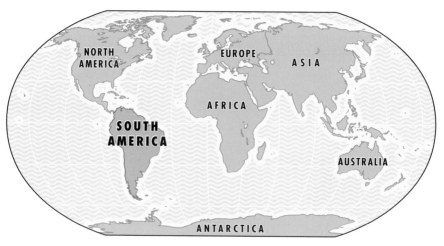

continents

globe

macaw

pampas

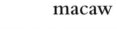

rain forest

31

Index

About the Author

Allan Fowler is a freelance writer with a background in advertising.
Born in New York, he now lives in Chicago and enjoys traveling.

Photo Credits

Photographs ©: International Stock Photo: 18 (Paulo Fridman); Liaison Agency,
Inc.: 20 (Wolfgang Kaehler), 27 (Ron Levy); Nance S. Trueworthy: 9, 31 top
left; New England Stock Photo: 23 (Chris Sharp); Photo Researchers: 22, 31
bottom left (Georg Gerster), 21 (David M. Schleser/Nature's Images, Inc.);
Robert Fried Photography: 4, 5; The Image Works: 14 (Wesley Bocxe), 29,
31 top right (Tom Brakefield), cover, 6, 30 right (M. L. Corvetto); Tony Stone
Images: 25 (Ken Fisher), 26 (William J. Hebert), 10, 30 left (Frans Lanting),
17 (Silvestre Machado), 13, 31 bottom right (A. B. Wadham).

Maps by Bob Italiano